DATE DUE			

3254716032316

970.0097
ENG

Englar, Mary.

French colonies in America

615595 02104   14655C   0001

We the People

French Colonies in America

by Mary Englar

Content Adviser: Richard J. Bell, Ph.D.,
Assistant Professor, Department of History,
University of Maryland

Reading Adviser: Alexa L. Sandmann, Ed.D.,
Professor of Literacy, College and Graduate School of Education,
Kent State University

Compass Point Books ◆ Minneapolis, Minnesota

Compass Point Books
151 Good Counsel Drive
P.O. Box 669
Mankato, MN 56002-0669

On the cover: Indians and French trappers meet to trade furs in 17th-century Montreal; color engraving, 1891, after Frederic Remington

Photographs ©: The Granger Collection, New York, cover, 5, 11, 12, 13, 24, 33, 34; Prints Old and Rare, back cover (far left); Library of Congress, back cover, 15; Bridgeman Art Library/Getty Images, 4, 38; akg-images, 7; North Wind Picture Archives, 8, 10, 17, 18, 19, 22, 23, 25, 30, 35, 37, 39, 40; Archives de la Manufacture, Sevres, France/Archives Charmet/The Bridgeman Art Library, 9; North Wind/Nancy Carter/North Wind Picture Archives, 16; *Bartering for a Bride* by Alfred Jacob Miller, Courtesy of the Eiteljorg Museum of American Indians and Western Art, Indianapolis, 21; Mary Evans Picture Library, 27, 28; Anthony Hernandez/iStockphoto, 31; Steven Miric/iStockphoto, 41.

Editor: Jennifer VanVoorst
Page Production: Bobbie Nuytten
Photo Researcher: Svetlana Zhurkin
Cartographer: XNR Productions, Inc.
Library Consultant: Kathleen Baxter

Art Director: LuAnn Ascheman-Adams
Creative Director: Keith Griffin
Editorial Director: Nick Healy
Managing Editor: Catherine Neitge

Library of Congress Cataloging-in-Publication Data
Englar, Mary.
  French colonies in America / by Mary Englar.
     p. cm. — (We the people)
  Includes index.
  ISBN 978-0-7565-3839-2 (library binding)
1. Canada—History—To 1763 (New France)—Juvenile literature. 2. Mississippi River Valley—History—to 1803—Juvenile literature. 3. French—North America—History—Juvenile literature. 4. France—Colonies—America—Juvenile literature. 5. North America—History—Colonial period, ca. 1600–1775—Juvenile literature. I. Title. II. Series.
  F1030.E54 2009
  970.0097'541—dc22   2008007209

Visit Compass Point Books on the Internet at *www.compasspointbooks.com*
or e-mail your request to *custserv@compasspointbooks.com*

TABLE OF CONTENTS

NEW FRANCE

On July 24, 1534, a band of sailors straggled ashore on a new land. Under the command of navigator Jacques Cartier, the 61-man crew had spent nearly three weeks crossing the Atlantic Ocean from their native France. King Francis I wanted some of the wealth that Spain had found in Mexico and South America. He had hired Cartier to

Jacques Cartier encountered new lands and people across the Atlantic Ocean.

search for gold and other precious metals that he believed could be found in North America as well. Cartier and his crew explored the coast of North America and sailed into what is now the Gulf of St. Lawrence.

They came to land on the Gaspé Peninsula. There Cartier erected a large wooden cross on the shore and claimed the land for France. He had not found gold, but he had gained his country a foothold in the New World. France would remain for more than 200 years, and its claims would grow to cover

Cartier claimed much of eastern Canada for France.

5

nearly all of the eastern half of North America.

However, for many years after Cartier claimed land in what would come to be known as New France, there were no colonists to live in it. In 1541, France tried to establish a colony along the St. Lawrence River, but it was a failure. Within a year, all the colonists had either died or returned to France. For the next 60 years, France limited its interests in the region to fishing expeditions off the Atlantic Coast. This changed in the early 1600s. The French had become interested in the fur trade. Europeans had overhunted most animals in Europe, and fur pelts were valuable. Fox and mink fur was used to trim the clothing of kings and wealthy nobles. Beaver fur was used to make popular hats. Fur pelts earned good prices for traders.

France decided to set up fur-trading posts in North America to trade with the American Indians. In 1604, French explorer Pierre du Gua, Sieur de Monts, founded a settlement in the territory of Acadia in order to establish a monopoly on the fur trade in the region. It was the first

The relationship between the French and the Indians was based on the trade of fur pelts.

permanent French settlement in North America. Acadia

included the present-day Canadian provinces of Nova

Scotia, New Brunswick, and Prince Edward Island, as well

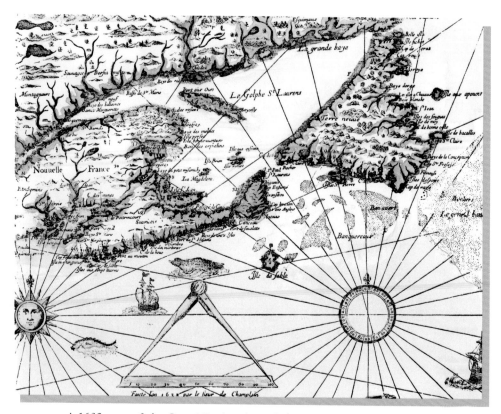

A 1632 map of the Gaspé Peninsula and the Gulf of the St. Lawrence features the land that was known as Acadia.

as part of the state of Maine. Acadia occupied territory that was also claimed by England. This led to frequent unrest, and Acadia changed hands many times over the next 150 years.

CANADA

Samuel de Champlain was a French explorer, soldier, and mapmaker. He had spent years exploring the Atlantic coast of North America and had taken part in founding a settlement in Acadia in 1605. In 1608, he led an expedition to build a fur-trading post in the St. Lawrence River Valley, a region known as Canada. Champlain chose a site along the St. Lawrence River that he described as "good land covered with trees, such as oaks, cypresses, birches, fir-trees and aspens, and also wild fruit-bearing trees, and vines; so that in my opinion, if this soil were tilled, it would be as good as ours." He called the new settlement Quebec.

Samuel de Champlain founded the city of Quebec to establish fur trade in the region.

Quebec also overlooked a good harbor at a place where the St. Lawrence River narrowed. The traders could travel farther to the west on the river to trade with Indian nations. It was far from the Atlantic coast, where traders from many different countries competed for furs. Plus, animals trapped in cold climates had especially thick and valuable fur.

On earlier voyages, Champlain had learned that trade with American Indians created friendships that helped both the French and the Indians. By exchanging metal tools, beads, and weapons, the French gave the Indians useful goods to

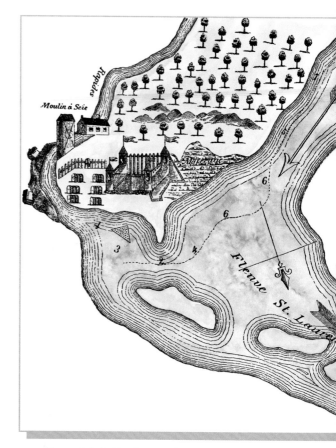

Champlain's Quebec settlement was located on a peninsula in the St. Lawrence River.

10

French fur trader Medard Chouart, Sieur des Groseilliers, greeted Native American allies while exploring in Canada.

improve their farming and hunting. In return, the Indians gave the French fur pelts, food, and help in traveling in a dangerous, unfamiliar world.

The first year at Quebec, Champlain and 27 men built a small fort on the banks of the St. Lawrence River. They hoped to stay warm that winter after their ship returned to France. Unfortunately, the men became sick with scurvy, a disease caused by the lack of vitamin C. By spring, only eight men survived. Champlain knew he would need help from the Indians to survive the winters and increase the fur trade.

In 1609, Champlain called the leaders of the nearest Indian nations to a meeting at Quebec. The Montagnais

Champlain invited the local Indian tribes to his Quebec fort for a meeting.

from the north, the Huron from the west, and the Algonquin from the Ottawa River sent warriors and leaders to the meeting. Champlain told them he wanted to build a settlement at Quebec. He needed their help to protect the small settlement and to bring fur pelts for trade. The three nations agreed to form a trade alliance with Champlain.

An 1891 engraving of French fur traders and their Indian trading partners

In return, Champlain agreed to help his allies defeat the powerful Iroquois to the south.

The alliance kept the colonists who arrived safe. The Huron were expert farmers and traded corn and vegetables with the new colonists. Members of all three Indian nations traveled far into the Great Lakes country and brought back large numbers of beaver pelts. They taught the French how to make canoes, fight scurvy, and stay alive through the long winters when the St. Lawrence River froze.

The colony grew very slowly. New France still seemed too dangerous and cold to most people back in Europe. In addition to Quebec, colonies had been founded at Trois-Rivieres in 1634 and at Montreal, then known as Ville-Marie, in 1642. Yet by 1660, New France only had 3,000 colonists. In contrast, 58,000 colonists had settled in the English colonies along the Atlantic coast.

In 1663, King Louis XIV took over the government of France's North American colonies. The king needed more soldiers and colonists to stop British colonists from

King Louis XIV was known as Louis the Great or the Sun King.

settling on land claimed as New France. For the next
10 years, the French government paid immigrants to move
to North America. Most of the men arrived as soldiers or

The royal banner of France featured the fleur-de-lis, which became the symbol of French rule in the New World.

indentured servants. They also worked as farmers or as servants for the priests and nuns of the Roman Catholic Church. These men did the hard work of clearing fields, building, and loading ships.

King Louis offered more than 750 women the chance to immigrate to New France. Those women who agreed were called the "king's daughters." Most of these women were orphans, and most were under the age of 25. The government paid for their voyage and offered them a small amount of money to marry quickly. Many of these women chose a husband, married, and went out to farm within a month of arriving.

By 1700, Canada was home to more than 15,000

French immigrants to Canada enjoyed a dance.

colonists. King Louis' plan had helped increase New
France's population, but England's immigration continued
to exceed that of the French.

THE UPPER COUNTRY

Throughout the 1600s, France continued to expand its territory. West of the St. Lawrence Valley, France claimed most of the land around the Great Lakes and along the major rivers. They called this land the Upper Country. Though the French claimed to own this land, the American Indians who lived there saw them as traders and protectors, but not as owners.

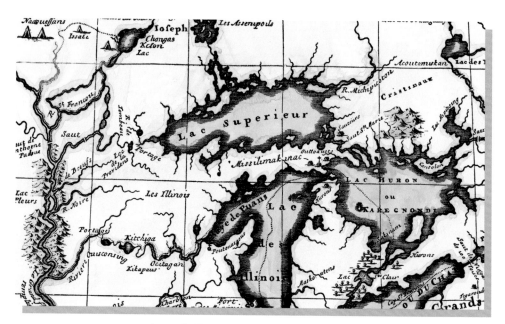

An early French map of the Great Lakes and Upper Mississippi

The westward expansion of France's North American empire was prompted by the decline of the fur trade in the St. Lawrence Valley. Some traders traveled to the Great Lakes to find new trading partners. They built trading posts and forts in the area and made alliances with various American Indian nations. They depended on their Indian allies to bring them pelts. The French also needed their allies to protect their trade from other European and Indian traders.

An Upper Country trapper made his rounds.

19

It was dangerous work, and many traders died each year. The best traders learned some Indian languages, and some married Indian women. By becoming part of a village or tribe, the traders brought valuable trade goods to their Indian families, and the Indians protected these traders as they would their own families.

As trade grew, the French built forts on important rivers and lakes to protect their trade rights. Fort Detroit, which later became the present-day city of Detroit, was one such location. Most of the trading posts were weeks away from the main colonies in the St. Lawrence Valley. The French king appointed a military governor, a civil administrator, and a Catholic bishop to run the New France colonies. Of the three, only the Catholic bishop and his missionaries had much power in the Upper Country.

From the first days of New France, the church had sent missionaries to teach the American Indians about the Roman Catholic religion. This religion was accepted as part of life by the French king and most French people.

Alfred Jacob Miller depicted the wedding of a trapper and an Indian woman in an 1847 painting.

The missionaries believed that the Indians needed to accept the Catholic religion or they would not go to heaven when they died.

The missionaries traveled all over the Upper Country

French missionaries relied on area trappers for advice and assistance.

with traders. They learned the Indian languages so they
could talk about their religion. Many American Indians
saw the missionaries as pests. Others welcomed them
into their villages. The missionaries built churches in the

Roman Catholic missionaries preached to Native Americans and fur traders alike.

Indian villages and taught those who wanted to learn about their religion.

The spread of European diseases was an unexpected consequence of the close contact between the French and the Native Americans. Traders, explorers, and missionaries carried diseases such as smallpox and measles. The French did not get as sick from these illnesses, but the Indians died

Diseases such as smallpox spread thoughout Indian villages, killing thousands.

in huge numbers. In the 1630s, more than 10,000 Indians died after the missionaries set up churches in their villages.

The French never colonized the Upper Country as they had the St. Lawrence Valley. By 1750, just 2,000 colonists and 261 soldiers lived at the trading posts of the Upper Country. The government of France built the posts and sent soldiers to protect their land. The government did not expect to build large settlements, but they needed to protect their territory from the increasing numbers of British colonists looking to claim new land.

THE LOUISIANA TERRITORY

French explorers and missionaries continued to travel farther west and south on important rivers such as the Illinois, the Ohio, and the Mississippi. In 1673, Louis Jolliet, a fur trader, and Father Jacques Marquette, a missionary, were the first Frenchmen to explore the Mississippi River. Soon other explorers followed the river the Indians called the "father of waters."

In February 1682, French explorer René-Robert Cavelier, Sieur de La Salle, set out with a group of

Father Marquette raised a peace pipe to signal his peaceful intentions.

25

20 Frenchmen and 30 Indians to explore the Mississippi River. He planned to canoe to the mouth of the river at the Gulf of Mexico. It took two months for his group to paddle from the Illinois River to the mouth of the Mississippi. La Salle claimed all of the land along the Mississippi River, from the Great Lakes to the Gulf of Mexico, for France. He also claimed the land along all the rivers that emptied into the Mississippi. La Salle named this vast new French territory Louisiana in honor of King Louis XIV.

In 1684, La Salle led an expedition from France to found a colony at the mouth of the Mississippi River. However, he got lost and sailed past the mouth of the Mississippi. His ships landed west of the river at Matagorda Bay on the Texas coast in 1685. There he established the colony of Fort Saint Louis. The new settlement was a dismal failure. Nearly 320 colonists died from disease and starvation within two years. His own followers killed La Salle in 1687.

After this failure, it took more than 10 years for the French to return to the mouth of the Mississippi. In 1698,

La Salle claimed the lower Mississippi for King Louis XIV of France.

explorer Pierre Le Moyne, Sieur d'Iberville, set out from France with three ships. He brought enough men, supplies, and livestock to build a fort on the Gulf Coast.

Iberville reached the mouth of the Mississippi River the following year. The water was too shallow to allow

27

ships to come and go. Instead, Iberville chose Biloxi Bay in present-day Mississippi and built Fort Biloxi. He returned to France to get approval from the king for more colonists. He left his brother Jean-Baptiste Le Moyne, Sieur de Bienville, behind as the deputy commander of Fort Biloxi.

A reproduction of a 1702 map by Iberville of North America

28

In 1702, Iberville built a second fort on Mobile Bay in present-day Alabama. The French king wanted to be sure that the French could defend Louisiana from the British colonists in the Carolina Colony. Iberville formed alliances with Choctaw and Chickasaw Indians who shared the land north of the Gulf of Mexico. He offered these allies guns and ammunition in exchange for deerskins. When Iberville saw that the Louisiana colonies were strong, he left his brother, Bienville, to govern Louisiana.

The colony grew slowly. In 1708, fewer than 300 colonists lived in Louisiana. In 1717, the king gave the Company of the Indies the right to colonize Louisiana. The company decided that the fertile Mississippi Valley would be better for farming. Bienville founded the city of New Orleans in 1718. In 1722, the company moved the capital from Biloxi to New Orleans to be closer to the plantations they hoped to create.

Over the next 20 years, the Company of the Indies sent 5,400 colonists and 6,000 enslaved Africans to Louisiana.

Settlers arrived with shiploads of provisions to establish their plantation settlements.

The company gave land to the colonists to encourage settlement. Most farms were located along the Mississippi River. Farm families worked the land alone, unless they had enough money to buy slaves or indentured servants. Most raised tobacco and indigo to sell in Europe.

A house built by French settlers is one of only two surviving structures from the founding of New Orleans.

The new colonists were not used to the region's hot, humid summers. Many died of malaria. The land was swampy and flooded every spring. Clearing land was difficult in the tropical climate. Nearly two-thirds of the colonists died or left by 1731. Those who stayed worked hard to improve their farms and plantations. By 1745, 3,300 colonists, 4,100 slaves, and 600 soldiers lived in Louisiana.

THE FRENCH AND INDIAN WAR

By the mid-1700s, French colonial leaders worried about the growing British colonies in the east. In 1754, New France had about 70,000 colonists. The British colonies

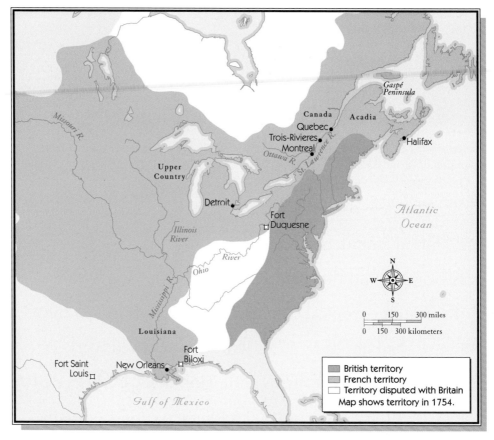

France's huge territory in North America was sparsely populated.

were home to 1.5 million colonists. The French were badly outnumbered, as well as being spread out from Canada to the Gulf of Mexico.

Between 1689 and 1748, Britain and France had gone to war in Europe three times. The conflict had spilled over into their colonies in North America, and the fear and distrust between the French and British colonists grew. Acadia changed hands several times during this period, and in 1713 it was turned over to Britain once and for all. At the end of King George's War (1744–1748), the British built a naval base at Halifax, Nova Scotia. In response, the French built new forts in Nova Scotia and along their trade routes in the Upper Country.

Acadian settlers were forcibly removed from their land by British soldiers.

33

The French had been forced to surrender the fortress of Louisbourg during King George's War.

In 1754, the major battles between Britain and France moved to North America. Britain wanted to expand its presence on the continent by taking over New France. The war to control North America broke out at the headwaters of the Ohio River. The French believed the Ohio Valley belonged to them. The British colonists in Virginia wanted the fertile land, too. The French sent soldiers to an area called the Forks of the Ohio. They captured a British trading post and began to build Fort Duquesne to protect their trade on the Ohio River. They planned to fight to keep British colonists out of the Ohio Valley.

The British colony of Virginia sent a small company of soldiers to challenge the French at Fort Duquesne. George Washington, a young officer in the colonial militia, led the British colonists. Washington's men attacked a small group of French soldiers on patrol near the fort. The French sent a larger group of soldiers and Indians to attack Washington. The large number of French soldiers and Indian warriors forced Washington to surrender. Washington and his men were allowed to return home to Virginia. This battle marked the beginning of the French and Indian War (1754–1763).

Colonel George Washington attacked French forces in a ravine during the French and Indian War.

THE SURRENDER OF NEW FRANCE

In the early years of the French and Indian War, New France had many victories. It had an organized military and many Indian allies. The French again defeated the British military at Fort Duquesne in 1755. Then they captured and destroyed two British forts in New York. Their Indian allies took many prisoners there, terrifying the British colonists.

In 1756, Britain and France again went to war in Europe, mainly because of the conflict in North America. The following year, William Pitt became the new prime minister of Britain. He sent more troops and warships to North America. British ships kept French supply ships from reaching the St. Lawrence colonies.

At the same time, the St. Lawrence colonies suffered poor harvests. Without fresh supplies from France, the French colonists and soldiers were starving. Pitt had sent

The French and their Indian allies ambushed the British near Lake George, New York, in 1755 during the French and Indian War.

many more soldiers than France. By 1758, the British had 45,000 British and colonial soldiers. The French had fewer than 10,000 soldiers, but they had more Indian allies to help them.

37

The French relied on their Native American allies to help them fight the British.

Nevertheless, over the next year, the French suffered many losses. By 1759, the stronger British troops were approaching the St. Lawrence Valley from the west and south and had entered the St. Lawrence River in the east. France was also busy fighting Britain overseas in the West Indies, India, and Africa, as well as in Europe. New France was not as important as their valuable colonies in the West Indies.

It took three months in 1759 for the British to capture the walled city of Quebec. The French cities of Montreal and Detroit soon followed. The French had been defeated in North America. However, fighting continued in Europe and around the world until 1763. At the end of the war, France signed the Treaty of Paris and gave up its land in North America east of the Mississippi River. In return, the British let France keep its valuable West Indies colonies on the islands of Guadeloupe, Martinique, and St. Lucia.

In its 200 years in North America, France

The English defeated the French at Quebec to capture the walled city.

never made money from its New France colonies. The French government paid settlers to move there, but the fur trade never completely paid them back.

France's Indian allies suffered more. French traders and colonists had not moved many Indians off their lands. After the war ended, however, British colonists flowed into the Ohio Valley and cleared land without asking the Indians. British troops stayed at Detroit and other trading posts they had captured. They were not interested in

Chief Pontiac urged Native Americans to fight British expansion.

forming alliances with the Indians, and the Indians had no European ally to help them protect their lands.

Although New France disappeared in 1763, many French traditions continue in Canada and the United States. Quebec Province in Canada has many people who still speak French at home and at work. New Orleans is home to many cultures, including some people who still speak French. From Louisiana to Montreal, French names for cities, lakes, and rivers have survived to remind North Americans of these early settlers.

Montreal street names pay tribute to its French history.

41

GLOSSARY

alliance—agreement between nations or groups of people to work together

foothold—position usable as a base for further advance

indentured servants—people who work for someone else for a certain period of time in return for payment of travel and living costs

indigo—plant that produces a deep-blue dye

malaria—disease that causes fever and chills; it is spread by the bite of mosquitoes that carry the disease

missionaries—people who travel to new lands to spread their religion

monopoly—right, granted by a court, to conduct business without competition

pelts—animal skins with the fur still on them

plantations—large farms in the South, usually worked by slaves

Roman Catholic—Christian church that is headed by the pope

Did You Know?

- The Native Americans whom Jacques Cartier met during his explorations lived in a village they called Kanata. Cartier thought the word referred to the whole region, and so the whole area along the St. Lawrence River became known as Canada.

- Acadia's location at the mouth of the St. Lawrence River was attractive to the British. The thousands of Acadians who settled there were forced to leave during the French and Indian War. Some of them settled in Louisiana and are known today as Cajuns.

- In the 2001 Canadian census, just over 7 million Canadians spoke French as their first language. This is about 24 percent of Canada's population.

- In 1762, France gave Spain the western portion of the Louisiana Territory as payment for Spain's assistance during the French and Indian War. France reacquired the land from Spain in 1800 and sold it to the new United States of America in 1803. This sale, known as the Louisiana Purchase, doubled the size of the United States.

IMPORTANT DATES

Timeline

1534	Jacques Cartier claims land in North America for France.
1604	Pierre du Gua, Sieur de Monts, founds the colony of Acadia.
1608	Samuel de Champlain founds Quebec.
1663	King Louis XIV takes over the government of France's North American colonies.
1682	René-Robert Cavelier, Sieur de La Salle, claims Louisiana Territory for France.
1718	Jean-Baptiste Le Moyne, Sieur de Bienville, founds the city of New Orleans.
1754–1763	The French and Indian War is fought in North America and overseas.
1763	The Treaty of Paris ends all French claims to North America.

IMPORTANT PEOPLE

SAMUEL DE CHAMPLAIN (1567?–1635)
French explorer and mapmaker who explored Acadia and the St. Lawrence Valley between 1603 and 1635; founded Quebec in 1608 and is often called the "father of New France"; during a 1609 raid on the Iroquois, he became the first European to reach Lake Champlain, which he named for himself

PIERRE LE MOYNE, SIEUR D'IBERVILLE (1661–1706)
French-Canadian trader, soldier, naval officer, and explorer; took part in many expeditions against the English, capturing or destroying many English forts; after La Salle failed to find the mouth of the Mississippi River from the Gulf of Mexico, Iberville located it in 1699 and set up forts at Biloxi and Mobile in Louisiana Colony; he died in the Caribbean while campaigning against the British

RENÉ-ROBERT CAVELIER, SIEUR DE LA SALLE (1643–1687)
French trader and explorer; as a young man in France, he had studied to be a priest; after moving to Montreal, he became a wealthy fur trader and explorer who traveled down the Illinois River to the Mississippi River and on to the Gulf of Mexico; he founded Fort Crevecoeur, the first European settlement in present-day Illinois; in 1682, he claimed the huge territory of Louisiana for France

45

WANT TO KNOW MORE?

More Books to Read

Blashfield, Jean F. *Cartier: Jacques Cartier in Search of the Northwest Passage.*
Minneapolis: Compass Point Books, 2002.

Heinrichs, Ann. *La Salle: La Salle and the Mississippi River.* Minneapolis:
Compass Point Books, 2002.

Moore, Christopher. *Champlain.* Plattsburgh, N.Y.: Tundra Books, 2004.

Parker, Lewis K. *French Colonies in the Americas.* New York: PowerKids
Press, 2003.

Thompson, Linda. *The Great Lakes.* Vero Beach, Fla.: Rourke, 2006.

On the Web

For more information on this topic, use FactHound.

1. Go to *www.facthound.com*

2. Type in this book ID: 0756538394

3. Click on the *Fetch It* button.

FactHound will find the best Web sites for you.

On the Road

Colonial Michilimackinac

102 Straits Ave. W.

Mackinaw City, MI 49701

231/436-4100

Restored fur trade village and fort in northern Michigan with re-enactments of a French wedding and the arrival of fur traders

Quebec City Fortifications

100 Rue Saint-Louis

Quebec City, Quebec

Canada G1K 7A1

418/648-7016

National Historic Site with three miles (4.8 kilometers) of historic city walls surrounding old Quebec

Look for more We the People books about this era:

African-Americans in the Colonies

The California Missions

Dutch Colonies in America

English Colonies in America

The French and Indian War

The Jamestown Colony

The Mayflower Compact

The Plymouth Colony

The Salem Witch Trials

Spanish Colonies in America

The Stamp Act of 1765

The Thirteen Colonies

Williamsburg

Women of Colonial America

A complete list of We the People titles is available on our Web site:
www.compasspointbooks.com

INDEX

About the Author

Mary Englar is a freelance writer and a teacher of English and creative writing. She has a master of fine arts degree in writing from Minnesota State University, and has written more than 30 nonfiction books for children. She lives in Minnesota, where she continues to read and write about the many different cultures of our world.